Other books by Rene' Gordon

Who? What? When? Where? How? Why?
A Story about a Life

The Next 31 Days:
Realign Your Thinking, Realign Your Life

Animals In Our World: A – Z

...and more

Copyright 2004
Reprint 2018
ISBN 978-1-7329254-0-3 Print
ISBN 978-1-7329254-2-7 eBook

All rights reserved. No part of this book may be reproduced or transmitted in any form or by
any means, electronic or mechanical, including photocopying, recording, or by any
information storage and retrieval system, without permission in writing from the copyright
owner.

Publisher:

ReneWritesBooks
Website: www.renewritesbooks.com
Email: renewritesbooks@gmail.com

About Me

I've learned a lot of lessons in life. Some were the growing pains of a Black girl growing up in the south, and some were just the growing pains of a girl. I was fortunate to find a way to release my emotions through writing. It began with the need to express my feelings and grew into a desire to show the world "ME". I've had some ups and downs, just like any other person. Whether happy or sad or somewhere in between, these are my feelings of life, love, and loss. Hopefully you can get something out of it. Enjoy!

Table of Contents

Chapter 1: Life — 1
One Magical Moment — 3
Proud to Be Me — 5
Computer World — 7
Mistakes of Yesterday — 9
Somehow — 11
The Horizon — 13
Influence — 15
Color — 17

Chapter 2: Love — 19
To Have and to Hold — 21
Questions — 23
Solitude — 25
Never Been That Way — 27
In Love Again — 29
Wait — 31
From Me to You — 33
Child of Mine — 35
My Love — 37
Thorny Rose — 39

Chapter 3: Loss — 41
To You in Time of Need — 43
Always — 45
Be Lost in Me — 47
Looks Like Rain — 49
What's Wrong? I'm Just Tired — 51
Is It Time to Go Yet? — 53
Irony — 55

Life

One Magical Moment

I was looking outside my window at some trees
and the sky and rooftop of the house next door.
For a second or two, I was back in time, a déjà vous of some sort.
Something about the way the wind was blowing,
swaying the leaves and limbs of trees back and forth.
I could see my dog in the yard, even though she really wasn't there.
I could smell the warm grass and the air of late summer.
It was all too real, so real that I believed that if I were
to walk outside the door, I would actually be back there again.
A young, innocent child playing in the sun
with her dog happily jumping and dancing around her.
I wanted so badly to escape back to that time,
that time when I believed in so much and knew so little.
But I was so engulfed in this special, magical moment
of mystical recollection
that I dared not move for fear of disappointment of reality.
So I lay there, lost in time with a few seconds of a
special, secret, and satisfying memory.

Proud to Be Me

If I were an eagle,
I'd soar to the highest peak.
I would be a symbol of power.

If I were a lion,
I'd roam about my jungle.
I would be a symbol of strength.

If I were a star,
I'd shine brightly in the heavens.
I would be a symbol of hope.

If I were a lens,
I'd see the world for what it is.
I would be a symbol of justice.

If I were a lamb,
I'd stand in snow white wool.
I would be a symbol of innocence.

I am a human being.
I am a creation of the Almighty.
I am a symbol of life.

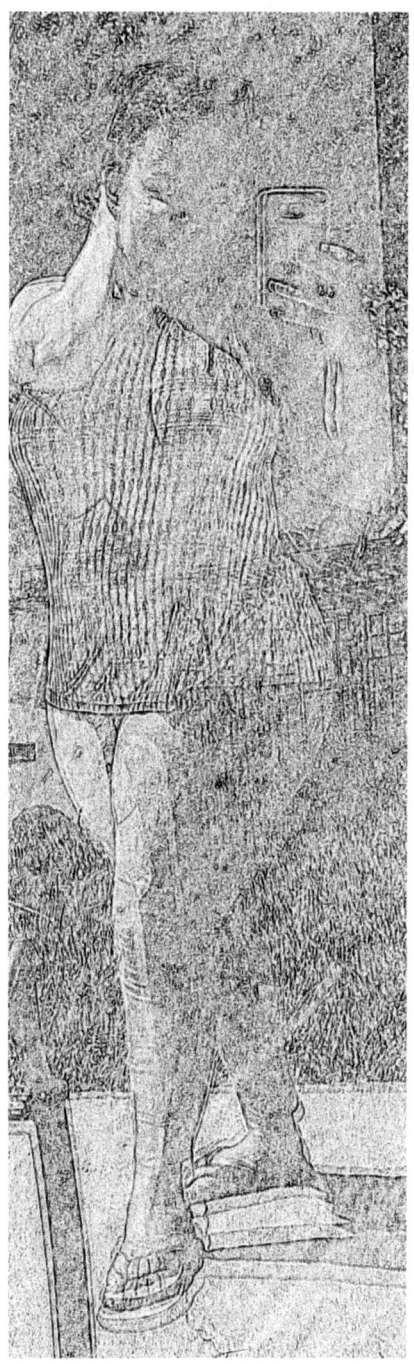

Computer World

If people were like computers,
and we had arrows to move forward and back,
we could use the "HELP" function
to find the knowledge we lack.

We could change our current format
to whatever we want it to be.
We could even click on "FIND"
to see what we needed to see.

We could save our current workbook
to preserve that moment in time.
And we could set up warnings
to alert us of danger with a chime.

Life would be so simple
with just 1's and 0's to guide us.
And when we needed a break from our day's work,
we could just set up a macro to hide us.

The best part of it all
that would be oh so sweet
is if we made a mistake
we could just backspace or delete.

Mistakes of Yesterday

Memories of yesterday, of times not far behind, but long gone.
Never to be again, and I wish I had it all to do over.
We all make mistakes and wish we could go back to some time before and have a second chance.
Can we really do anything any differently this time, or will we repeat ourselves each time making the same mistakes?
If it were any different than what it was, then we wouldn't be who we are today.
Our reactions and actions, mistakes and misfortunes, pain and heartache, and even the good things, be them few, all shape our lives and make us who we are or who we were.
No one escapes sadness, pain, or love…not even a child.

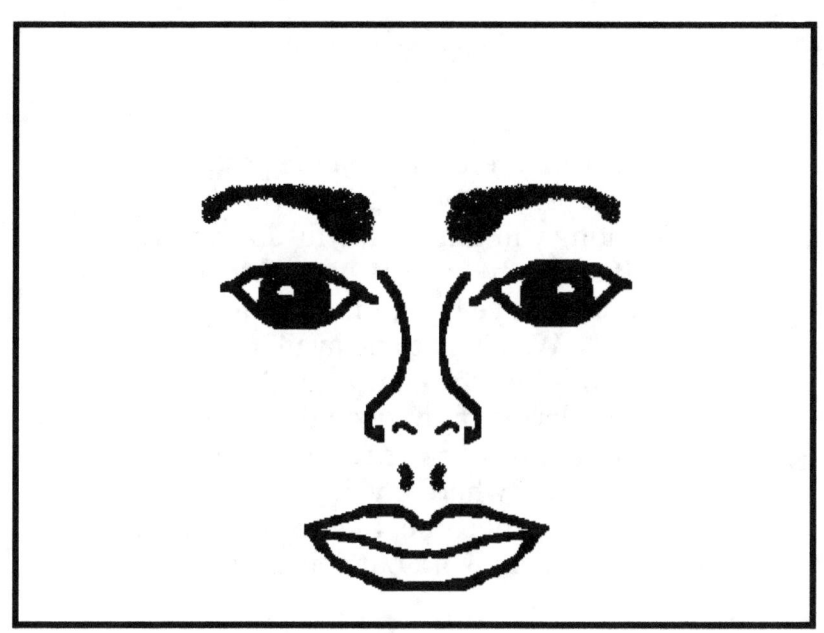

Somehow

Sitting, reflecting on the past,
I question my value and worth.
How long will this sorrowful stage last?
It seems to have begun at birth.
At times I've fought for my rights.
Was it all to no avail?
At times I've stayed up half the night
wondering if love would prevail.
Now all that is over with and gone forever.
I know where my life is now.
I know what will come. I know the weather.
It will all work out somehow.

The Horizon

Upon the horizon
the sun sits low.
This is the place
to where I must go.
I'll sit on the hilltop
in solitude.
No longer will my words
be misconstrued.
At peace with myself
I shall be.
My life will finally
have harmony.
My destiny is
not far away.
No longer am
I led astray.
I know the road
on which I travel
will lead me home.
My life I've unraveled.
This beautiful place
which lies ahead
is to whom
I will be wed.
Forever shall I
remain here.
With no more sorrow
and no more fear.

My earthly possessions
I've left behind
Now I will have
a clear state of mind.
I finally understand
what life is about.
No longer do I
have any doubts.
I've had to struggle
all my life,
but along this journey
there is no strife.
It was worth it all.
Nothing was in vain.
All happiness
I have regained.
All faith and innocence
will return.
This is for what
I deeply yearn.
When I reach
my journey's end,
everlasting love
will engulf me then.
This is the purpose,
this is the reason,
my destiny lies
upon the horizon.

Influence

Influence only results in an echo, echo, echo.

Your soul is passed on to another.

Your thoughts are stolen from you brain.

Your sins become those of your admirer.

Everything you do and say is imitated.

You are not yourself anymore.

Someone has stolen your identity.

You no longer exist in the world as yourself and your shadow has taken over your life.

Be yourself and let no other change you.

Color

If I were a black bird,
I'd fly to the highest mound.
If I were a white bird,
I'd not let my wings touch ground.
But I am a gray bird, so
I'm somewhere in between.
I'm as proud as a black or white bird
and still soar to reach my dreams.

Love

To Have and to Hold

When I think of you
    what comes to mind
        I cannot quite explain.
            Though barely friends
              I'm wanting more.
                  Yet friends we must
            remain.
Thoughts and desires
    all starring you.
        I'll keep them to myself.
            For the disasters of trying
              too hard too soon
                  I know of far too well.
I'll take my time.
    I'll keep my cool.
        I'll take each day in stride.
            While passion burns
              each time we kiss,
                  I'll keep so much
              inside.
Afraid I'll push you
    away from me,
        these feelings remain untold.
            Yet the truth be known
              it's you I want
                  to have and to hold.

Questions

Sitting, staring, studying
your moves, gestures, mannerisms.
Are you alone or with someone?
I can't quite determine.
Wondering, wanting, waiting
to see you again, or will I ever
Who are you?
Where do you live?
Time, today, tomorrow, an
eternity passes.
Where are you?
Will I ever see you again?
No, this was just once in a lifetime.
Then slowly, sexily, stealthily you
move towards me.
Where have you been?
Why did you stay away so long?
Carefully, cautiously, cunningly
I plan an encounter.
What are you thinking?
Do you like me?
Plotting, planning, perpetrating
just to see you again.
Do you want to see me?
Do you find me attractive?
Testing, talking, teasing
one another.
Finally in touch.
Are you thinking what I am?
Do you like me too?
Encounter, erotic, enticing
kissing that drives me wild.
Why are you here?
What do you want?
Is it just a game?
While sitting, I wonder, while time slowly passes.
I'm plotting, while testing you.
Another encounter?
Many, I hope.

Solitude

Alone I sit in solitude
while sad and painful feelings brood.
Too painful to remember,
Yet too meaningful to forget,
So deeply set.
In my mind are all the
thoughts of then.
A time of way back when.
Actually it's of a time
not too long ago.
I'll never forget them though.

Never Been That Way

They sing songs of love and walking holding hands.
They tell stories of lovers in near and distant lands.
Things like truth and honesty,
Tell me why can't there be one song or story that tells of me.

I've read poems that say I want and need you near.
I've always hoped that someday these words I would hear.
"You're the only one I need",
"There is no one else for me",
"Baby I love you", and it would really be true,
but hope is all I ever do.

I've never felt the love that the songs all sing about.
I've never had my love returned and knew without a doubt
that as much as I had loved, love was returned to me.
It's never been that way for me.

Romantic fairytales and daydreams have been my company.
So now it's all clear to me
that I may never feel love that the songs all sing about.
I may never have my love returned and know without a doubt.
So much as I love, love is returned to me.
It may never be that way for me.

In Love Again

I've been in love, or so I thought,
a time or two before.
It didn't last for long and
always left me wanting more.
I said I'd never love again
and then I found in you a friend.
So when will I be ready to fall in love again.

I've hurt so long and so deeply,
and thought I'd never feel
the things I'm beginning to feel for you.
And yet it seems so unreal.
For these feelings I didn't plan,
yet I don't want them to end.
So when will I be ready to fall in love again.

Could you be feeling these things too?
Dare I express my thoughts to you?
I don't want things to move too fast.
That's happened too often in the past.
Oh how I want this friendship to last.

Love again, in love again.
When will I be ready to fall in love again.
Feels like my heart will never mend.
So when will I be ready to fall in love again.

And now I know you feel the same
because you told me so.
This new relationship we have
we both now can explore.
No more hiding tears in the rain,
trying to disguise the pain.
because I think I'm ready to fall in love again.

Love again, in love again.
I think I'm ready to fall in love again.
It takes time for hearts to mend.
I think I'm ready to fall in love again.
Yes, I know I'm ready to fall in love again....with you.

Wait

When we're together, now and then, it's hard to contain
emotions that lie deep within, and yet I must remain
controlled, composed, serene and calm.
Though time and time again
I think that there would be no harm
in us being closer than just friends.

I know you share these feelings too for you have told me so.
But I agree that what we should do
is first let our friendship grow.
Two people sharing passion's fire
is natural to enjoy.
But shared too soon, lust and desire,
our friendship it would destroy.

Be there for me and I there for you
in weakness and temptation.
For now friendship we should pursue
to strengthen our relations.
Should you become doubtful and insecure
and giving up you contemplate,
passion still grows so rest assured
good things come to those who wait.

From Me to You

It isn't enough to love.
It isn't enough to need.
It isn't enough to want
and ache with each heartbeat.

It isn't enough to laugh.
It isn't enough to cry.
It isn't enough to smile
when inside I slowly die.

I give to you my mind.
I give to you my heart.
I give to you my life
and yet we're still apart.

I bring to you sadness.
I bring to you pain.
I bring to you confusion
and your tears pour out like rain.

You can keep my love, my need, my want,
my laugh, my cry, my smile, my mind,
my heart, and my life.

I'll take away your sadness,
your pain, and your confusion,
and I'll hurt you no more.

Child of Mine

You have my blood, my face, my hair and my eyes.
I give to you my wisdom, my courage, and my hard-learned lessons.

You have my smile, my nose, and my attitude.
I give to you my story, my heritage, and my knowledge.

You have my laugh, my silly ways, and my kind-heartedness.
I give to you my sense of direction, my keen awareness, and my love for music.

You have my hands, my feet, and my knobby knees.
I give to you my optimism, my desires, and my hopes.

You have so much of me in your looks.
I give to you all of me in my love.

My Love

My love for you will last forever.
My love will live eternally.
And when the angels sing for me
my love will sing for you.

My heart I give to only you.
For you my heart will only beat.
And if you give your heart to me
I'll cherish it always.

And with the dawn of every morning,
And when I lay my head to sleep,
I'll pray that you'll be here with me
'cause I'll be here for you.

There is no other love for me.
My love I give to you only.
And if you'll give your love to me
I'll be yours forever my love.

Thorny Rose

You came into my world and turned it cold.
Your face is pale and eyes are black as coal.
Your tongue is forked and heart is made of stone.
Your mind is narrow and you're much too bold.
You are so young but your lies are so old.
You always return confusion a thousand-fold.
I never would have loved you if I had known.

Why did I have to meet you?
I wish I'd never crossed your path.
If I knew then, what I know now, it would be a different story.

I guess all good things must come to an end, it's true.
I do still love you. I only wish you loved me too.

Loss

To You in Time of Need

The loss of someone close to you
I will consider my loss too.

We all are affected when one is gone.
Grief comes into all our hearts and homes.

To you my sympathy I will lend,
and also know you have a friend.

Though our hearts are shattered and shaken
by this loss, let us not be mistaken.

We have lost one in body, but you see,
through the heart, one gains immortality.

Always

Tears fall down my window pane
in the form of silent rain.
The thunder crashes.
The pain grows stronger.
My heart drowns in self-made sorrow.

        A streak of lightning reaches out
        and searches, searches round about.
        I am found.
        I can hide no longer.
        Pity just isn't the answer.

What can I do to break away?
I just can't bear it another day.
Why does it have to be this way?
It's just not fair at all.
We'll never know what could've been.
At least in you I've found a friend.
If only we could go back again.
I don't want to leave.

        Minute details are magnified.
        For once my eyes are open wide.
        The captured, released.
        The hidden, unveiled.
        I see things I've never seen before.

Life now means so much more.
I wish I could reopen the door.
Don't take it for granted.
Live, laugh, and love.
You weren't promised a tomorrow.

        I'm sorry that I must say goodbye,
        but please, my friend, do not cry.
        Always hold your head up high.
        We'll be together someday.
        As long as I am in your heart,
        I promise you we'll never part.
        Intertwined souls is what we are
        because I love you and always will.

Be Lost in Me

So it ends, the final chapter of a tragedy.
Death is always a romantic resolution.
A sorrowful hand shames the act by giving it a touch of irony.
A letter of confession adds to the sorrow and regret.
A love poem deepens the passion and the feeling of loss.

For now sleeps the crimson petal.
Now folds the lily, all her sweetness up
and slips into the bosom of the lake.
So fold thyself, my dearest thou, and slip into my bosom
and be lost in me.

Looks Like Rain

Looks like rain today.
Some clouds are forming ahead.
Like my Grandma used to say,
"good day to stay in bed".
But I've got lots of things to do,
some errands to run and things.
Life has to go on too,
Even if rain is what the day brings.
So let the clouds fill the sky,
And let that old rain flow.
I'll wipe my face dry,
and onward I will go.

What's Wrong? I'm Just Tired.

I'm tired of always laughing
when I really want to cry.
I'm tired of still living
but I'm too afraid to die.
I'm tired of always pretending
that everything's okay.
I'm tired of always feeling pain
each and every day.
I'm tired of always loving
and needing love too.
I'm tired of feeling like a failure
in everything I do.
I'm tired of always holding on
yet still having to let go.
I'm tired of always asking, begging
yet still hearing "no".
I'm tired of feeling alone
even in a crowd.
I'm tired of having to hide my tears
and not being able to cry out loud.
I'm tired of hurting others
and having others hurt me.
I'm tired of looking for happiness
when there's nothing there to see.
I'm tired of being here.
I just want to go away.
I'm tired of talking now.
I have nothing else to say.

Is It Time to Go Yet?

Is it time to go yet?
I've been in here a while.
It's dark, it's cramped, it's awful damp.
But I feel her smile.
Is it time to go yet?
It's crowded in this place.
I'm cold, I'm wet, haven't been fed yet.
Who is this in my face?
Is it time to go yet?
Why don't they leave me alone?
They've tickled and teased and even squeezed.
I wish they'd all go home.
Is it time to go yet?
I hear that place is fun.
There are games to play,
and alphabets to say,
and snacks for everyone.
Is it time to go yet?
There's so much for me to do.
New friends to greet, deadlines to meet,
and meetings to schedule too.
Is it time to go yet?
Didn't seem like that long a time.
So now I'll go skiing on the snow,
or sip some Caribbean wine.
Is it time to go yet?
The sun is going down.
Getting chilly outside. I'm kinda tired.
I think I'll go lie down.
Is it time to go yet?
Don't cry now, no, you hush.
Just let me say, live for today.
You don't have to rush.

Irony

Sunny days and blue skies did remind me of you...now, pain inside.
The love we shared, holding your hand, and gazing in your eyes...
...that's all I wanted to do.
That's what we had.
Always talking together and so in love we were.
One day of stormy weather...and then you went to her.
And since that day, my life had been so changed.....for the better.

Life is precious, love is beautiful, and loss can be overwhelming. Live in the present, love with all your heart, and know loss is just a part of life.

www.ingramcontent.com/pod-product-compliance
Lightning Source LLC
Chambersburg PA
CBHW052118070526
44584CB00017B/2537